BALTIMORE RAVENS

BY BO SMOLKA

SportsZone
An Imprint of Abdo Publishing
abdopublishing.com

abdopublishing.com

Published by Abdo Publishing, a division of ABDO, PO Box 398166, Minneapolis, Minnesota 55439.

Printed in the United States of America, North Mankato, Minnesota
042016
092016

THIS BOOK CONTAINS RECYCLED MATERIALS

Cover Photo: Damian Strohmeyer/AP Images
Interior Photos: Damian Strohmeyer/AP Images, 1; G. Newman Lowrance/AP Images, 4-5; Eric Bakke/AP Images, 6-7; NFL Photos/AP Images, 8-9; Al Golub/AP Images, 10-11, 14; Mark Humphrey/AP Images, 12-13, 15; Allen Kee/AP Images, 16; Elise Amendola/AP Images, 17; Tom DiPace/AP Images, 18-19; Gail Burton/AP Images, 20; Chris Gardner/AP Images, 21; Winslow Townson/AP Images, 22-23; Nick Wass/AP Images, 24-25; Matt Slocum/AP Images, 26; Patrick Semansky/AP Images, 27; Rick Scuteri/AP Images, 28-29

Editor: Patrick Donnelly
Series Designer: Nikki Farinella

Cataloging-in-Publication Data
Names: Smolka, Bo, author.
Title: Baltimore Ravens / by Bo Smolka.
Description: Minneapolis, MN : Abdo Publishing, [2017] | Series: NFL up close | Includes index.
Identifiers: LCCN 2015960329 | ISBN 9781680782080 (lib. bdg.) | ISBN 9781680776195 (ebook)
Subjects: LCSH: Baltimore Ravens (Football team)--History--Juvenile literature. | National Football League--Juvenile literature. | Football--Juvenile literature. | Professional sports--Juvenile literature. | Football teams-- Maryland--Juvenile literature.
Classification: DDC 796.332--dc23
LC record available at http://lccn.loc.gov/2015960329

TABLE OF CONTENTS

MILE HIGH MIRACLE

Things were looking bleak for the Baltimore Ravens. They trailed the Denver Broncos 35-28 with less than a minute left in their National Football League (NFL) playoff game on January 12, 2013. The Ravens were 70 yards from the end zone.

Center Matt Birk, 77, directs traffic as the Ravens battle the Broncos in the playoffs on January 12, 2013.

FAST FACT

Through 2015, Joe Flacco had led the Ravens to seven road playoff wins. That is the most of any quarterback in NFL history.

With Broncos linebacker Von Miller, *58*, closing in on him, Ravens quarterback Joe Flacco launches "The Mile High Miracle."

Ravens quarterback Joe Flacco dropped back to throw. Speedy receiver Jacoby Jones raced down the right sideline. Flacco lofted a high, deep pass through the frosty Denver air. Broncos safety Rahim Moore drifted toward the ball, but it sailed over his fingertips and landed softly in Jones's hands. The stunned crowd watched Jones run the final few yards for the game-tying touchdown.

Rookie kicker Justin Tucker's 47-yard field goal in the second overtime period gave the Ravens a 38-35 victory. They went on to win their second Super Bowl title. It would not have happened without the throw known as "The Mile High Miracle."

BALTIMORE COMES BACK

Baltimore has long been a great football town. The people there loved their Colts, who began playing in 1953. Some of the greatest players in the history of the National Football League made their names in Baltimore.

The Colts spent 31 years playing in Memorial Stadium. It started to get rundown, and the Colts' owner wanted a new stadium. Politicians refused to cooperate. So in March 1984, the Baltimore Colts bolted out of town, bound for Indianapolis. Fans were stunned and heartbroken.

FAST FACT

Before the Ravens came to town, Baltimore briefly had a Canadian Football League (CFL) team. The Baltimore Stallions won the Grey Cup, the CFL championship, in 1995.

Baltimore Colts fans once packed Memorial Stadium—shown here in 1960—but eventually the team left for Indianapolis.

Baltimore got its new NFL team much in the same way it lost the Colts. The Cleveland Browns' stadium was crumbling. The team was losing money. Maryland officials promised to build a new stadium in Baltimore for the Browns. So after the 1995 season, Browns owner Art Modell moved his team to Baltimore. They began playing as the Ravens in 1996.

The Ravens went 4-12 that first season. However, led by their first two draft picks—tackle Jonathan Ogden and linebacker Ray Lewis—better things were soon to come.

Quarterback Vinny Testaverde and the Ravens got off to a rough start in 1996.

SUPER DEFENSE

The Ravens hired Brian Billick as coach in 1999. He was an offensive-minded coach. But it was their smothering defense that turned them into champions.

The Ravens opened the 2000 season with a 16-0 shutout of their biggest rivals, the Pittsburgh Steelers. That was a sign of things to come. The Ravens recorded four shutouts and held five other teams to 10 points or fewer. They allowed only 165 points all season, the fewest ever in a 16-game season. Baltimore finished 12-4 and made the playoffs for the first time.

Jamal Lewis and the Ravens were hard to stop in the 2000 season.

FAST FACT

Rookie running back Jamal Lewis rushed for 1,364 yards in 2000. He set an NFL record with 295 rushing yards in a 2003 game.

In the playoffs, the bone-rattling defense again led the way. In three American Football Conference (AFC) playoff games, the Ravens allowed a total of 16 points. They forced five turnovers in a 16-3 win over the Oakland Raiders in the AFC Championship Game. In their first trip to the playoffs, the Ravens were headed to the Super Bowl.

Ravens kicker Matt Stover, *3*, led the NFL with 35 field goals in 2000.

Ray Lewis celebrates his interception return for a touchdown in the Ravens' playoff win over the Tennessee Titans.

The brash Baltimore defense stole the spotlight during the week before the Super Bowl. Linebacker Ray Lewis, safety Rod Woodson, and defensive tackle Sam Adams earned Pro Bowl berths. Everybody wanted to interview witty defensive tackle Tony Siragusa and confident cornerback Chris McAlister. On Super Bowl Sunday, those players went out and lived up to the hype.

The Ravens defense forced five more turnovers and did not allow a touchdown in a 34-7 thumping of the New York Giants. As the leader of Baltimore's dominant defense, Ray Lewis was named the game's Most Valuable Player (MVP).

Quarterback Trent Dilfer prepares to take the snap in the Ravens' Super Bowl victory over the New York Giants.

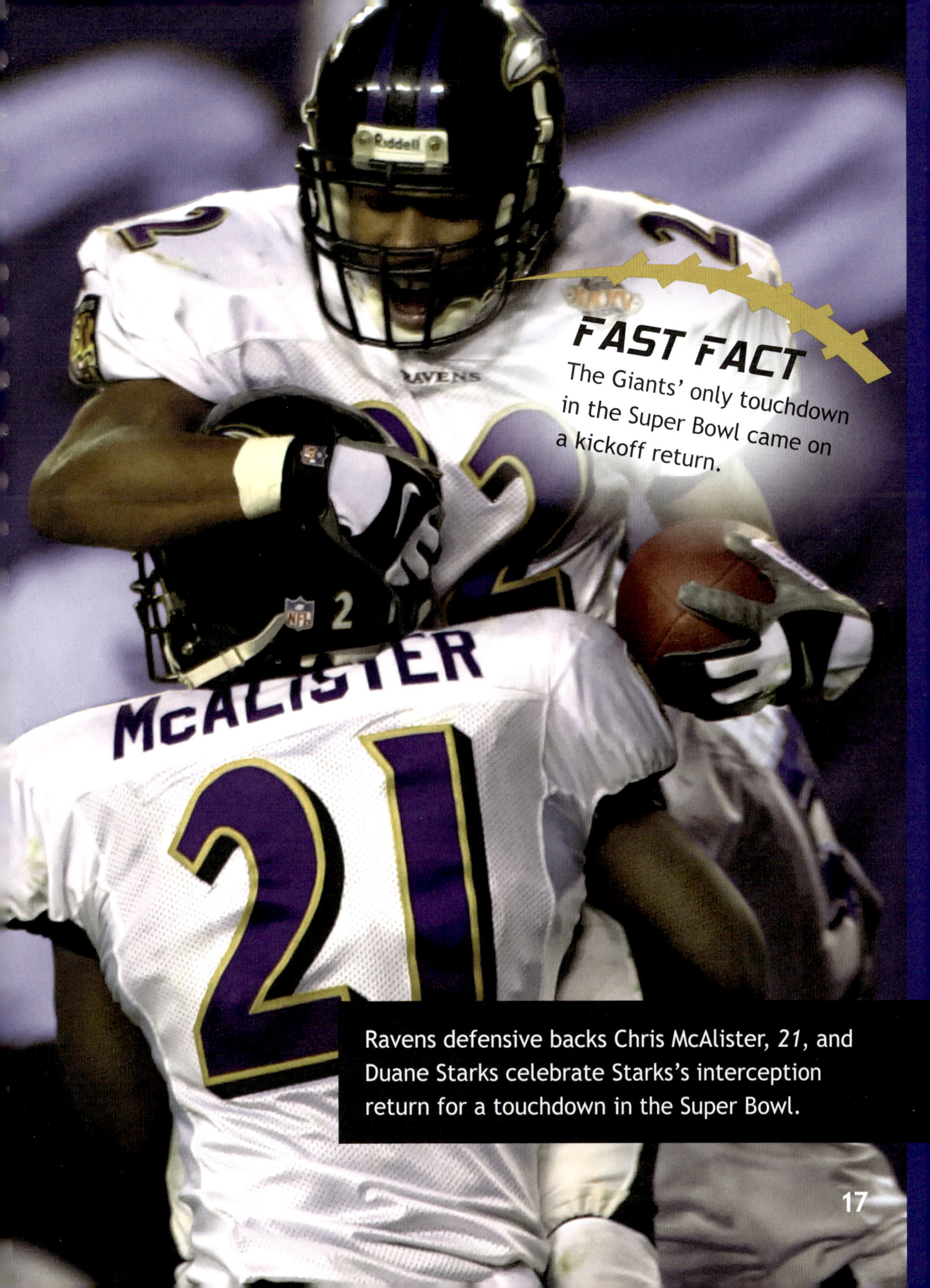

FAST FACT

The Giants' only touchdown in the Super Bowl came on a kickoff return.

Ravens defensive backs Chris McAlister, *21*, and Duane Starks celebrate Starks's interception return for a touchdown in the Super Bowl.

RAVENS
5
Art

A NEW ERA

A new era began for the Ravens in 2008. The team hired coach John Harbaugh and drafted quarterback Joe Flacco in the first round. They proved to be a winning combination.

Joe Flacco and John Harbaugh have had a lot to celebrate since they arrived in Baltimore together in 2008.

The Ravens reached the playoffs in each of Harbaugh's first five seasons. Flacco led the offense, while linebacker Ray Lewis and safety Ed Reed maintained the outstanding defensive tradition.

But getting to the playoffs was the easy part. Returning to the Super Bowl would prove to be much more difficult.

Ed Reed, *20*, heads up the field with one of his 64 career interceptions.

Linebacker Terrell Suggs, *right*, was a big part of the Ravens' great defenses.

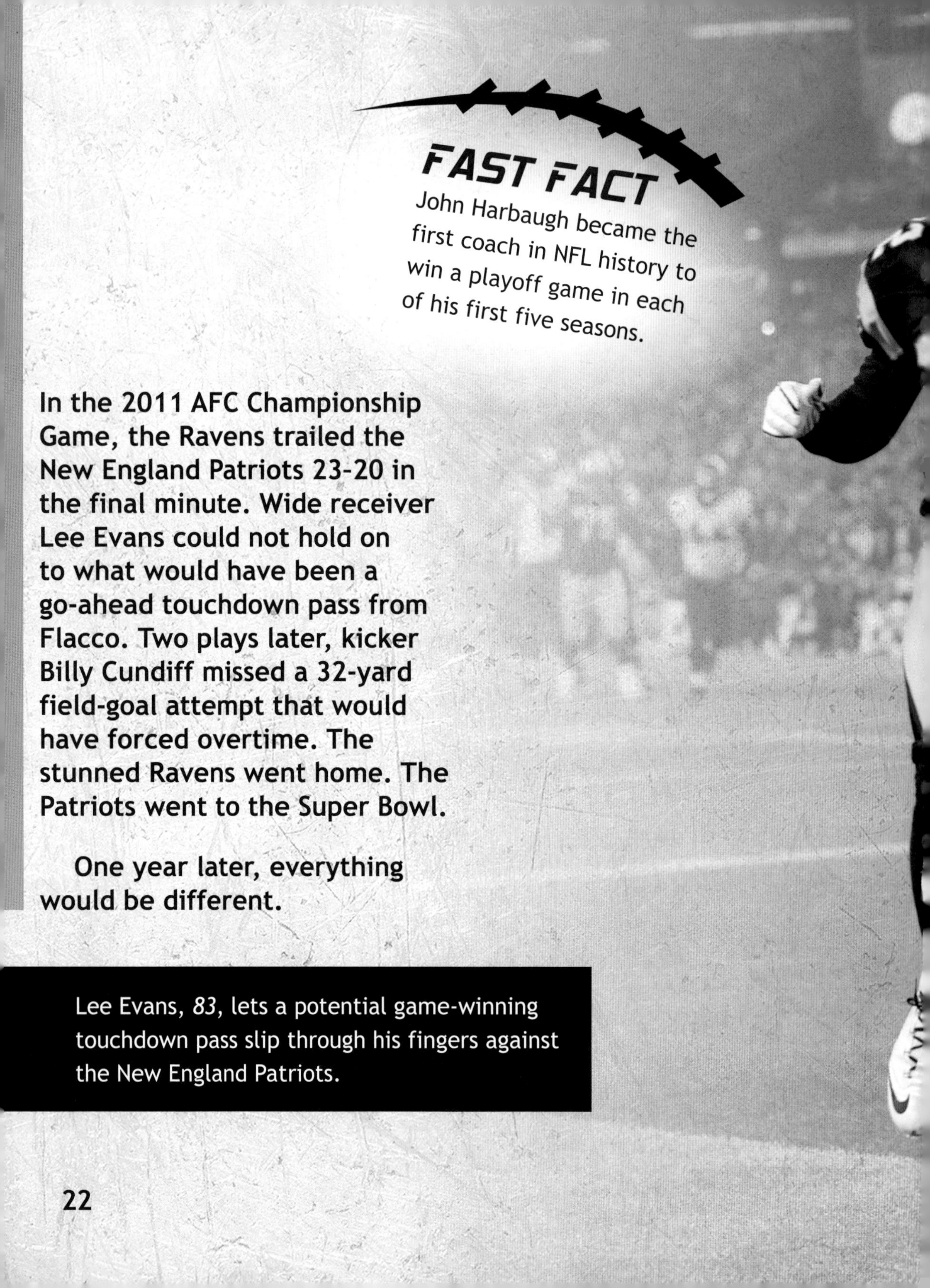

FAST FACT
John Harbaugh became the first coach in NFL history to win a playoff game in each of his first five seasons.

In the 2011 AFC Championship Game, the Ravens trailed the New England Patriots 23-20 in the final minute. Wide receiver Lee Evans could not hold on to what would have been a go-ahead touchdown pass from Flacco. Two plays later, kicker Billy Cundiff missed a 32-yard field-goal attempt that would have forced overtime. The stunned Ravens went home. The Patriots went to the Super Bowl.

One year later, everything would be different.

Lee Evans, *83*, lets a potential game-winning touchdown pass slip through his fingers against the New England Patriots.

Riddell
RAVENS
83

FAST FACT

Ray Lewis played 17 seasons, all in Baltimore. He was a two-time NFL Defensive Player of the Year. The Ravens placed a statue of Lewis outside their stadium.

BACK ON TOP

In 2012, the Ravens won the AFC North. Before the playoffs began, linebacker Ray Lewis announced he would retire at the end of the season.

Motivated by Lewis and led by Joe Flacco, the Ravens were unstoppable in the playoffs. The Mile High Miracle set up a rematch with New England in the AFC title game. This time, Baltimore rolled to a 28-13 win. They were back in the Super Bowl, where they faced the San Francisco 49ers.

Ravens linebacker Ray Lewis reacts to the crowd during the final home game of his career on January 6, 2013.

The Ravens led 28-6 after Jacoby Jones returned the opening kickoff of the second half 108 yards for a touchdown. Then electrical problems caused a long delay. When the lights came back on, the 49ers came storming back. But the Ravens' defense snuffed out a late San Francisco drive. Baltimore held on to win 34-31.

Ravens coach John Harbaugh, *left*, chats with 49ers coach Jim Harbaugh before the brothers' teams squared off in the Super Bowl.

Jacoby Jones sprints toward the end zone with the second-half kickoff in the Super Bowl against the San Francisco 49ers.

FAST FACT

Ozzie Newsome built the Ravens' roster as the team's general manager. Before that, he was a Hall of Fame tight end with the Cleveland Browns.

In the 2014 playoffs, the Ravens lost another close game at New England. Injuries took their toll in 2015, when the team slumped to a 5-11 record. Flacco missed the last six games after suffering a serious knee injury. And their first-round draft pick, wide receiver Breshad Perriman, missed the entire season with a knee injury. It seemed that injuries were the only thing that could slow down the Ravens.

Injuries to Joe Flacco and other important players derailed the Ravens' season in 2015.

54
54
CARDINALS
5
RAVENS

TIMELINE

1995
Cleveland Browns owner Art Modell announces he will move his team from Cleveland to Baltimore.

1996
The Baltimore Ravens officially begin play with a 19-14 win over the Oakland Raiders on September 1.

1998
The Ravens move into the stadium now known as M&T Bank Stadium after playing their first two seasons at Memorial Stadium, former home of the Baltimore Colts.

1999
Brian Billick is hired as coach on January 19. He goes on to compile a record of 80-64 with one Super Bowl championship over nine seasons.

2000
The Ravens finish 12-4 and set an NFL record by allowing 165 points, the fewest ever in a 16-game season.

2001
On January 28, the Ravens beat the New York Giants 34-7 for the first Super Bowl title in franchise history.

2004
Steve Bisciotti buys the Ravens from Modell.

2008
John Harbaugh is named coach. In the first round of the draft, the Ravens select quarterback Joe Flacco.

2013
The Ravens beat the San Francisco 49ers 34-31 on February 3 to win their second Super Bowl title.

GLOSSARY

BRASH
Self-assertive in a rude, noisy, or overbearing way.

FUMBLE
When a player with the ball loses possession, allowing the opponent a chance to recover it.

INTERCEPTION
When a defensive player catches a pass intended for an offensive player.

RIVAL
An opponent with whom a player or team has a fierce and ongoing competition.

SHUTOUT
A game in which one team does not score.

TURNOVER
Loss of the ball to the other team through an interception or fumble.

INDEX

ABOUT THE AUTHOR

Bo Smolka covers the Baltimore Ravens for Comcast SportsNet. He is a member of the Pro Football Writers of America and has written more than a dozen children's sports books. He lives in Baltimore with his wife and two children.